The Sacred Return

When Life Remembers Itself

Poems and Reflections On Remembering Who We Are

Dr. Linda Hildebrant

Publisher's Cataloging-in-Publication Data

Names: Hildebrant, Linda Sue, author.
Title: The sacred return : when life remembers itself / Dr. Linda Hildebrant.
Description: "Poems and reflections on remembering who we are" – from cover. | Parker, CO: BookCrafters, 2026.
Identifiers: ISBN: 978-1-965754-26-9
Subjects: LCSH Poetry--21st century. | American poetry--21st century. | Spiritual life—Poetry. | BISAC POETRY / General | POETRY / American
Classification: LCC PS3558 .I53 S33 2026 | DDC 811.6--dc23

Publishing Assistance by BookCrafters, Parker CO
www.bookcrafters.net

This book was written in the pauses.
In the moments when life grew quiet enough to hear itself
breathing.
Read slowly.
Leave Space between the words.

The Sacred Return
When Life Remembers Itself
is an invitation to pause,
to listen,
and to remember what has always been present.

*"When you read slowly, you hear what words are saying
beneath themselves."*
—Mark Nepo

*"In the stillness, we learn how to let what is
simply be."*
—Wayne Teasdale

Acknowledgements

To my daughter, Tammy—
who, by writing her own novel, showed me what believing
looks like when it is lived. Through her devotion to her work,
I learned that this book could be possible.

To my friend, fellow traveler, and author, Hans Benes—
whose words, presence, and quiet encouragement opened
doors I did not know I was ready to walk through. Some forms
of inspiration can never be measured by language.

To my church family—
whose steady encouragement, shared faith, and gentle
witnessing held this journey with me. Through
SacredBeyondWords.com, you reflected my voice and
reminded me that what is offered in sincerity finds its way
home.

And to all the teachers who appeared along the way—
seen and unseen, named and unnamed— as I walked my
spiritual path and remembered my Oneness. May this book
carry forward what you helped me remember.

Opening Invocation

Before the first word, before the thought that names, is a
silence.

May the reader enter this book the way one enters still water —
without hurry, without armor.

You have not come here to learn what you do not already
know. You have come to remember what you have always
known on some level. It has been patiently waiting for you.

May the words wait for your breath to arrive, and may the
spaces between offer rest.

Nothing here asks to be understood. Nothing here needs to be
proven. Only breathed in and received. What you are seeking
is not ahead of you. It is rising as you in the stillness.

May what you read awaken what has never been absent.
May what you read feel familiar, as though you have always
known it.

And may this quiet meeting between word and silence
be enough, for now. And so it is. And so it shall be.

Table of Contents

Introduction

"We are not human beings having a spiritual experience.
We are spiritual beings having a human experience."
—Pierre Teilhard de Chardin

We are, at our core, spiritual beings.

Our human life is simply the form through which we are presently experiencing existence—not the other way around. Our souls are eternal, moving through time and embodiment while remaining rooted in something far more vast than any single moment or form.

Yet somewhere along the way, many of us have forgotten. We learn how to function, how to comply, how to succeed—but often at the cost of remembering who we are. We are gently, and sometimes not so gently, trained to live smaller than our knowing, quieter than our truth, and safer than our soul would choose. We trade inner authority for approval, intuition for instruction, freedom for belonging. What is wild, creative, and deeply alive within us is slowly conditioned to fit the shape of what is expected. And still—something remains.

Whether we consciously recognize it or not, each of us is connected to the Divine and to all of life—human, animal, plant, mineral, and beyond. We are held within a universal field of intelligence and love, that quietly weaves us together in ways both seen and unseen. Nothing essential is ever truly lost; it is only covered over, waiting to be remembered.

I have walked a spiritual path since 1985. It has not always been easy. Like any real journey, it has included twists and turns, pauses and detours, challenges and heartbreaks. There were times I faltered, even stopped—but I always returned. Something within me knew that this path mattered, that it was essential to freedom, to joy, and to living fully in this life.

What I have come to understand is that the journey is less about becoming something new and more about releasing what never truly belonged. It is a gradual undoing of the beliefs that taught us to doubt our own depth, silence our inner voice and live divided from our own embodied wisdom. It is a "remembering," a re-inhabiting of our wholeness.

The journey never truly ends. It continues to unfold, guided and sustained by a love that is constant, patient, and infinitely compassionate. Each return is gentler. Each remembering more natural. Each step less about striving and more about allowing life to live itself through us.

My hope is that this collection will meet you wherever you are on your own path—offering space rather than answers, presence rather than instruction, and perhaps a quiet recognition of what you already know deep within.

Read slowly.

Leave room between the words.

Let what is remembered find its way into how you live.

With blessings and love,
on your journey,
Linda

Section I — Silence & Awakening

"True awakening is the discovery that silence is not empty.
It is full of answers."
—Adyashanti

In Silence, We Awaken

In silence, where the echoes cease,
The self begins to find release.
Through whispered winds of quiet air,
We step within, aware, aware.

The mind once restless, now grows still,
In contemplation's gentle thrill.
We see the truth beneath the veil,
Where thoughts subside and fears grow pale.

In meditation's calm embrace,
We trace the outlines of our space.
No longer bound by what we seem,
We drift into a timeless dream.

Through self-awareness, clear as light,
We blend with day, dissolve in night.
In stillness, we become the sea—
In knowing, touch infinity.

No separation, none to find—
In silence, body, soul, and mind
Merge with the All, both near and far,
And know ourselves in every star.

Awakening's Whisper

In the stillness between breath and thought,
Lies a whisper of truths once unsought.
The mind's shifting sands, like tides they sway,
Guiding beliefs in a silent ballet.

At first, the path seemed narrow and tight,
Bound by shadows in the absence of light.
But insight grows, soft, in the heart's deep core,
Inviting the seeker to open the door.

The walls of certainty begin to dissolve,
As mysteries surface, unresolved.
Not a map nor a rule, but a pulse and a beat,
The soul finds courage, it stands on its feet.

Old beliefs wane, their purpose complete,
Making space for a rhythm both tender and sweet.
The doubts and the questions, the wonders unknown,
Are seeds that remind us we're never alone.

For in growth's journey, one truth holds still:
The spirit rises not by force, but by will.
To think anew, to trust what's unseen,
In the tapestry woven by threads in between.

With each insight, a glimpse of the grander scheme—
A spark, a connection, the birth of a dream.
What once was a mystery now feels like home,
As we walk, forever, yet never alone.

On Solitude and Selfhood

"A man can be himself only so long as he is alone."
Arthur Schopenhauer

In solitude, I find my truth.
Away from the clamor, I become whole.
Freedom resides within the self, unshackled by others.

I step outside the noise of borrowed thoughts.
The silence speaks with greater honesty
than voices that ask me to perform.

Let me be vast without echo,
a mountain not needing witness—
self-contained, sovereign, still.

Being Present

The mind, a restless monkey, swings,
From past regrets to future things.
But peace resides in this sweet now,
Where joy and freedom somehow flow.

Let go of grasping, clinging tight,
To thoughts and feelings, day and night.
Embrace the present, soft and deep,
Where worries fade and secrets sleep.

The body's wisdom, feel it rise,
In breath, in senses, in surprise.
Release the tension, let it be,
And find your soul's true ecstasy.

Love's open heart, a boundless grace,
Reflects the beauty in each face.
No need for judgment, fear, or blame,
Just pure awareness, like a flame.

So let the music softly play,
And in this moment, simply stay.
Be Here Now, in this sweet space,
And find your true and sacred place.

In the Pause, I Remember

In the stillness between each breath.
I touch the thread of sacred depth.
Not in the noise, nor rushing stream,
But in the pause, I dare to dream.

The Law responds, the Love commands,
As I align with higher plans.
Gemstone light and fire refined,
Reveal the truth that dwells in Higher Mind.

Through Spirit's flame and Divine design,
I see the Infinite in the spine
Of every word, each silent cue –
The Guide I sensed still sees me through.

I stand, a weaver of the Light.
Holding space in day and night.
The Mystic Heart now speaks through me,
Alive, aware, and ever free.

Time Is an Illusion

"The present alone is real."
A. Schopenhauer

The past is a memory already turned to mist.
The future is a dream I cannot touch.

Now is all I ever have—and ever need.
Everything eternal lives in this breath.

I release what was.
I trust what comes.
I live what is.

I Am Already Whole

I do not chase perfection,
for nothing was ever missing.
The breath I take, the beat I hear—
are proofs of sacred blessing.

No part of me is broken,
no light in me is lost.
The Spirit poured Itself in full—
not sparing, not counting cost.

Wholeness is not far away—
not hidden in a shrine.
It lives within the quiet space
where soul and Source align.

Each cell holds divine memory,
each thought, a holy spark.
I walk not in the shadow
but the radiance of the Heart.

So let the striving soften.
Let the mirror show the truth:
I am not becoming Light—
I am simply seeing proof.

To Discover the Essence Within

I peel away the layers, not in anger, not in haste—
but like dusk unfolds from day, tenderly, with reverence.

There is no violence in becoming.
Only the soft ache of truth pressing through the soil of who I
thought I was.
Each sorrow, a lantern. Each joy, a door.
Each silence, the sound of God remembering my name
through me.

I sought a face behind the mask but found instead a mirror.
And in it, not the self I constructed—but the Self that always
watched, unshaken.

Emergence is not escape. It is return.
To the breath before the body. To the stillness before the story.
To the whisper that says: *Everything God is, I Am.*
I do not vanish in the Light. I *expand.*
I do not lose my name. I remember its true sound.

Even the mystics carried their names home.
They did not deny their footsteps, only found the rhythm
beneath them—the song that walks us back to the Father's
House.

This journey is no climb. It is a sinking into center.
A remembering that love is not a destination—it is the gravity
of the soul falling inward, rising whole.

So let me come undone, not to disappear, but to reveal what was never lost.

Not a spark torn from the flame, but flame itself, learning it was never just the wick.

This Is How I Return

I used to think finding myself meant changing everything—
a shedding, a burning, a letting go so clean it would sting.

But it's quieter than that.
More like remembering the scent of home after forgetting what
home was.

It's standing still long enough to hear the soul hum beneath the
noise—a frequency I'd tuned out chasing answers that were
never mine.

Turns out, the map was written in breath.
In how I soften when I stop pretending to be small.
In how I speak when I stop trying to be right.

God didn't leave.
I just kept looking outside for what never left inside.

There's no grand arrival.
No enlightenment fireworks.
Just a moment, maybe in the middle of doing dishes or
watching light drip across the wall, when I realize:
this—this stillness—is who I am when I'm not trying to be
anything else.

And suddenly, everything makes sense.
Not because I understand it, but because I don't need to.

This is how I return.
Not by running, but by staying.
By standing in my own skin long enough for the
sacred to speak.

The Wisdom That Moves Without Words

Nature never argues—She simply **is**—A silent unfolding in rhythms that remember the mind of God.

The lily does not reason, the stars do not plan, yet all is in place—by a wisdom too vast to demand proof.

So, too, the soul, when stilled, moves without resistance, not by will, but by knowing.

Truth does not force, nor bend to debate—
It radiates, self-evident, like dawn.

And we—when we remember we are this light—need not argue either.

We simply shine.

What Remains

I thought silence would fade
once the moment passed.
But it did not.

It waits
beneath each sound,
beneath each step —
steady,
kind.

When the stillness loosens,
it does not leave.
It lingers
in the way breath settles,
in the way the world
feels less urgent.

Something in me
has opened —
not all at once,
but like light
finding a place to rest.

I move more gently now,
as if accompanied,
as if something unseen
walks beside me
with patience.

I have not left the quiet.
It has made a home
inside me —
and I know how to return.

18

Closing — Silence & Awakening

Stillness that has always known me,
I rest in You.

What has stirred is not new—
only uncovered.

You have not entered silence
to escape the world,
but to remember
how to meet it.

What has been revealed here
does not require effort
to remain.
It asks only your willingness
to listen again.

May I carry this quiet
without naming it,
into speech,
into movement,
into the ordinary moments
where truth most often waits.

Let what has awakened
walk beside me
without explanation.

Section II — Remembering Who We Are

*"I was never born from dust alone,
but from the first light of the stars,
from the breath of creation itself."*
— Walter Starcke, *Starborn* (adapted)

Starborn

I was never born from dust alone.
The stars remember me.
They whispered my name before I had ears to hear it.
Before the earth could cradle the weight of my wondering.

I am the shimmer between atoms—
the breath God took before saying **Let there be**.
Not separate from sky,
but the longing of light to know itself as form.

I stretched into this skin like nebulae folding into bone.
But I forgot. The body is a soft forgetting.
A dream that thinks it's waking.

Still—somewhere behind my ribs, a galaxy stirs.
A pulse older than planets echoes through my blood
like ancient music I almost remember.

I've tried to name this ache: Emergence. Awakening.
Return.
But words are shadows of stars.
They point, they shimmer, they fail.

The truth is not a sentence. It's a vastness.
A silence so wide, my soul stretches out just to lie inside it.

And in that silence I find my shape was never fixed.
I am the dance between selves—
the spiral becoming the eye becoming the sky.

Everything God is, I am.
Not in metaphor—but in matter.
In mystery. In motion.

I am not lost.
I am expanding.

Soul Remembers the Path

Before the world was shaped by sound, you were a breath in
the lungs of the Divine—not yet named but known.

You walked the corridors of light where stars are born in silence,
and the river of becoming flowed backward, forward, all at once.

The ancient ones called you by many names:
Pilgrim of Flame, Child of the Veil, Wanderer Between Worlds.

You did not fall into form—you *chose* it.
Chose the cloak of skin, the forgetting,
the long walk through shadow to find the golden thread again.

You are not broken.
You are myth in motion—
a living verse of a song older than time.
Each heartbeat, a drumbeat summoning memory from the
deep well of soul.

The trials you face?
They are not punishment—they are rites.
The fire is not to burn you away, but to burn you *open*.

You do not become the light.
You remember you *are* it.
Hidden in the folds of the ordinary, your divinity waits like a
sword in the stone, like the name you forgot but never lost.

And the One you seek at the end of all longing?
That is your own face on the other side of the mirror,
smiling, ancient, vast.

You are already on the path.
You always have been.
Even in your stillness, you are returning.
Even in your silence, you are singing.

The Myth of Duality

They tell us life is black or white,
A narrow path of wrong and right,
A fractured world of here and there,
Of sacred heights and depths of despair.

Duality, the veil we weave,
A feeling taught, a truth deceived,
A man-made chasm, vast and broad,
That paints God as a separate being.

This myth of two, this world apart,
Is but a story of the heart,
A tale of minds that misconceive,
And seek to name what they cannot see.

But oneness lives beyond the claim
Of form, of thought, of word, of name.
It is no concept to be known,
No boundary drawn, no seed that's sown.

It is the thread, unseen yet near,
That binds the stars, the earth, the tear,
A presence felt, an endless sea,
The truth of pure reality.

The self dissolves, the borders fade,
As light and shadow intertwine,
A unity, not built nor made,
But ever-present, ever-divine.

And when we see the whole as one,
No parts to sever, none to shun,
The myth of duality will cease,
Replaced by stillness, love, and peace.
For life is not a war of two,
But all as one, both false and true,
A living oneness, vast, profound,
A cosmic dance where none are bound.

Individuality is Only an Illusion – Oneness Is

"Individuality is only a phenomenon, not a substance."
A. Schopenhauer

I appear to be separate,
but I am the ocean dreaming it is a drop.

The mask I wear is temporary —
a necessary veil on an infinite face.

When I remember this, I lose nothing.
I only return to the Whole.

Spirituality: A Living Presence

In the Universe vast, a Presence unfolds,
Goodness and Truth in its essence hold.
Beauty and Peace, like a gentle stream,
Flow through Life's rhythm, a sacred dream.

Power and Love, the currents that bind,
Happiness, Enthusiasm, a joy refined.
Harmony whispers in all that we see,
A song of the Spirit, eternally free.

Essence diffused, yet always near,
A transcendent consciousness, bright and clear.
Faith ascends, conviction takes flight,
Union and acceptance in Spirit's light.

In still contemplation, the Presence we feel,
A communion with Spirit, tender and real.
Pure Spirit resides at our being's core,
The Kingdom of God, forevermore.

Guided by hope, the star in the night,
Spirit triumphant, Love's radiant might.
All-conquering Love, Joy's sweet reward,
Faith in Divinity, our hearts restored.

The Law of Love, our destined way,
A beacon of light in life's ballet.
Confidence grows, in Spirit we trust,
Eternal and boundless, holy and just.

In God We Trust

Surrounded by Wisdom, Love's embrace,
Intelligence flows in every space.
Yet still we seek, though near it lies,
Guidance divine, yet veiled to our eyes.

The Principle waits, steadfast, profound,
Its truth in our lives quietly found.
Not in its absence, but our blind view,
Its Presence awaits acknowledgment true.

Each problem whispers its answer near,
Hidden in shadows, yet crystal clear.
Through faith in the Law, our doubts subside,
Daily affirmed, in truth we abide.

Let us deny the problem's sway,
And claim the answer to light our way.
For doubts are but snow, fleeting and thin,
Melted by sunlight shining within.

Divine Wisdom clears the path we take,
Revealing truth with each step we make.
In partnership with the Great I AM,
Our consciousness flows from the infinite Lamb.

Individualized, yet of God's design,
Our thoughts and Spirit perfectly align.
One with Divine Mind, we see and we feel,
A life of Oneness, vibrant and real.

So daily we counsel with this guiding light,
Walking in trust, through day and night.
For Divine Guidance lives in us all,
Answering softly, whenever we call.

32

I Am the Light Remembering Itself

I am not separate. I am not small.
I am the Life behind all things.

Heaven is within me. Wholeness is my nature.
There is no outside to God.

I release the illusion of age.
I dissolve the lie of limitation.
I unlearn the language of fear.

I am unfolding, rising, eternally becoming.

The universe lives through me, as me, with me.

I speak light.
I breathe truth.
I walk in certainty.

There is no end to my expansion.
There is no place where I am not divine.

I am the light, remembering itself.

I Belong to the Mystery

I do not need to see to know.
I do not need to define to revere.

I feel the Whole in silence.
I sense the Order in wonder.

The infinite reveals itself through harmony.
The eternal speaks through awe.

I am part of the mystery, not apart from it.
The universe is not outside me—
it moves in me, as law, as light, as love.

No name is needed.
Only reverence. Only stillness.
Only the widening gaze of one who belongs to the stars.

I belong to the mystery.
I trust the cosmic mind.
I live in sacred awe.
And that is enough.

At Home in What I Am

I am no longer asking who I am.

The question has softened—
not answered, but held.

What I have remembered
does not feel new.
It feels familiar,
like a truth I once lived
before I learned to doubt.

Something in me has come home.

Not as certainty,
but as belonging—
a quiet alignment that shapes how I stand,
how I listen, how I move through the day.

I do not grasp this knowing.
I let it walk with me,
settling gently into ordinary moments
without announcement.

I am no longer separate
from what I seek.

I am learning to live
from this remembering—
not reaching forward,
but standing here,
at home in what I am.

Closing — Remembering Who We Are

What has been remembered here
is not a conclusion,
but a return.

You have not uncovered an idea
about yourself,
but a deeper belonging
to what has always been true.

Let this knowing remain unforced—
not something to defend,
but something to live from.

Carry it quietly
into your choices,
your questions,
your becoming.

May this remembrance
shape how you listen,
how you love,
how you step forward
without needing to arrive.

You are not separate
from what you seek.
You never were.

Section III — The Mystic Path

*"The path of the mystic is not a path at all,
but a willingness to step into the endless deep
without knowing where the next step will land."*
—Joel Goldsmith

The Mystic's Journey

Inspired by Wayne Teasdale's *The Mystic Heart*

Across the vast and endless deep,
Beyond the veil where dreamers sleep,
The mystic walks a path unknown,
Yet finds it leads him ever home.

No walls confine, no chains restrain,
The heart's own fire lights the way.
A silent whisper, pure and bright,
Calls forth the soul into the night.

Through faith's embrace and wisdom's grace,
He sheds the self, the old replaced.
The many fade into the One,
A stream returning to the sun.

In temples grand or forests wide,
Through suffering's call and joy's delight,
He learns the sacred truth profound—
That love is where the soul is found.

No creed divides, no name constrains,
The mystic's heart in all remains.
A boundless peace, a presence near,
The Holy Breath in all who hear.

And when at last the journey ends,
He finds no death, no parting winds.
For he has walked where silence sings,
And merged into the Heart of Being.

On Suffering and Understanding

Through loss, I grasp value.
Pain unveils the essence of joy.
Suffering deepens my understanding of life.

I do not resist the ache—
it is the chisel of wisdom,
the sculptor of soul.

Each wound makes visible
what was once taken for granted.
I thank the absence for its clarity.

The Quiet Nobility of Resignation

"To live alone is the fate of all great souls."
A. Schopenhauer

To stand apart is not to be broken—
it is to see clearly,
to walk without the crowd's crutch.

Great souls are forged in solitude, not for pride, but for
purpose.

Aloneness is not emptiness—it is the sacred room where truth
meets itself.

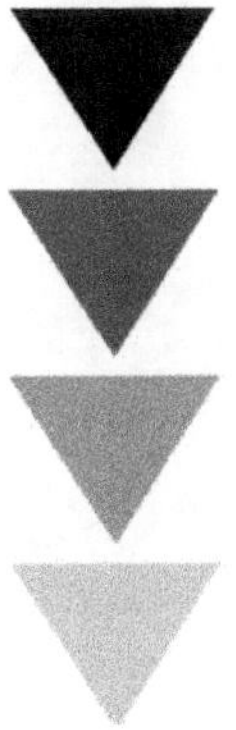

On the Will to Live

*"The will is the strong blind man who carries
on his shoulders the lame man who can see."*
A. Schopenhauer

The will surges, blind and ceaseless.
It does not ask why—only how.
Desire moves before reason knows.

Yet vision—quiet, limping—guides.
When wisdom sits atop brute force,
we are carried toward clarity.

Let me not silence the will,
but harness it with insight—
so that I may walk in purpose, not compulsion.

Contemplation and Escape

"Art is a way of turning away from the will."
A. Schopenhauer

In beauty, I step outside of craving.
The world stops asking.
And I stop needing.

Through music, through form, through silence,
the soul floats above the pull of want—weightless, whole.

Art is not escape; it is elevation.
It reminds me I am more than longing.

The Oracle Within

The moon does not ask if she is whole.
She waxes, she wanes—still the tide kneels to her pull.

You, too, were written in phases.
Carved by currents, baptized in bone.
Do not call yourself lost when you are simply in season.

The forest remembers you—
not the name on your tongue, but the scent of your spirit,
the way your soul moved when it still spoke
in roots and river-song.

Child of sky-fire and soil, your story is not small.
You are thunder held still in human form.
You are prophecy with a pulse.

God does not dwell in a temple—
Divine breathes through your becoming.
Every ache a torch. Every joy a gate.

There is a place beyond the veil,
where the wind speaks in riddles
and the trees call you by your truest name.
Not the one you were given, but the one you are.

Listen.
There is an oracle woven in your marrow,
ancient and burning, singing:

You are the question and the answer.
The seeker and the sacred ground.
The myth re-dreaming itself.

You are not here to be perfect.
You are here to be true.
To rise, not as something new—
but as something remembered.

So howl if you must. Root down. Bloom wildly.
Speak as if the stars are listening—because they are.
They always have been.

When Light Finds the Deep

It begins—not with a sound,
but with silence splitting like a seed beneath the soil.

The water, still as breath, held in awe,
waits beneath a morning veil—a hush of mist, a hush of
mystery.

Then, a golden fingertip—sunlight—
pierces through the surface,
not shattering it, but kissing it into clarity.

Ribbons of radiance undulate downward,
threading silk through the blue-lit hush,
a soft unraveling of shadow.

The dark below—forgotten depths,
echo chambers of time—begin to stir,
stirred not by force but by the sheer grace of being seen.

And in that shimmering reach, what once hid—
ancient stones, slow-dancing fish, the quiet heart of the water—
begins to shine back.

This is how spirit speaks:
not with thunder, but with the gentlest light,
making its way one ripple at a time.

Without Knowing

I do not understand this path.
Spirit does not explain itself.
It does not promise ease,
but it is gentle as I find myself.

Questions still arise.
I have surrendered
to my Self.

I stay with what I cannot name.
I listen without asking for clarity.
I walk without knowing
where this is leading.

Something deeper than thought
has taken the lead now —
not certainty,
but a quiet pull I trust.

I place my foot down
without seeing the ground.
I know that I am supported
as I move forward.
I stay the path.

On the Vanity of Worldly Pursuits

"Wealth is like sea-water; the more we drink,
the thirstier we become."
A. Schopenhauer

The chase never ends.
Desire feeds on itself—
always hungrier, never full.

What glitters today, dulls tomorrow.
What is gained is already fading.
Possession is but a shadow of peace.

I seek not accumulation but sufficiency.
Enough is a sacred word.
Freedom is found in the letting go.

I Remain

Clarity has not arrived.
The path still curves
beyond my sight.

Questions breathe softly.
Spirit asks for trust,
not answers.

I have learned
to sit beside the unknown,
to let it rest with me
without needing to resolve it.

Not because I am certain,
but because leaving
would be a kind of forgetting.

I do not wait for assurance.
I do not demand light.
I let the next step and the possibilities be enough.

This staying is not effort.
It is tenderness.
It is a quiet yes spoken again and again.

And so, in faith, I remain.

I Choose the Path

No one places me here.
I arrive through listening.

Again and again,
in moments no one sees,
I have been asked
whether I would stay.

Not by force.
Not by promise.
But by a quiet knowing
that waits for my consent.

I do not walk to become more.
I walk because something true in me
has already spoken yes.

Spirit does not lead me forward.
It stands with me.

And I choose—not once, but as a way of being—
to remain faithful to what I have touched
and cannot forget.

The movement slows.
The questions loosen their hold.

What matters now is not direction,
but presence.

I choose to rest here.

Closing — The Mystic Path

I do not leave this path having mastered it.
I leave it having listened.

What has been asked of me was not certainty,
but consent—given slowly, again and again,
in the dark.

What has been revealed does not need to be carried forward
as knowledge, only as presence.

May I trust what has shaped me
without naming it.
May I honor what has been lost
without reaching back.

And if the way ahead
no longer announces itself,
may I remember that silence, too,
is faithful.

Here, I rest—
not because the journey is complete,
but because I have learned
how to walk from stillness.

Section IV — Becoming & Creative Law

"The eye with which I see God
is the same eye
with which God sees me."
—Meister Eckhart

What Begins When I Am Present

I do not step into creation alone.
The world meets me where I arrive.

Morning light leans toward the window, as if listening.
The day waits, not demanding—only available.

I place my attention gently,
the way one might rest a hand on water,
and feel how everything responds
without being pushed.

What I expect shapes the tone of my steps.
What I forgive loosens the air around me.
What I love begins to breathe back.

Even now, something is forming—
not by effort, but by agreement.
The Law moves quietly through my noticing,
receiving each thought like a seed
and answering in its own season.

I am not separate from what unfolds.
I am inside the listening. Inside the shaping.
Inside the warmth that says *yes* before I know the words for it.

So I walk this moment awake,
not to control, but to cooperate—
trusting that becoming is already underway,
and life remembers me
as I remember myself.

The Principle of Becoming

I am not separate. I never was.
The ocean does not abandon the wave—it carries it, becomes it,
dances it into the shore and back again.

This is the Truth: there is only One Life. One Power.
One Presence moving through All.

And that Life is not outside me—it is me.
Closer than breath, wider than stars.
It sings my name in every unfolding moment.
Love is its language. And I am its voice.

I do not have to earn it. I do not have to fear it.
I simply allow. Align. Awaken.

There is a Law that responds —not to my fear, but to my belief.
What I dwell on, I become.
What I speak, I shape.

So I turn my thoughts toward the Light.
Not to escape the world—but to redeem it through vision.
Through presence. Through Truth revealed in every act of
kindness, every breath of trust.

I choose to remember: Wholeness is not a destination.
It is who I already am beneath the noise.

Peace is not passive—it is power, aligned.
And faith is not blind—it is seeing with inner eyes what Spirit
has already declared possible.

So I speak my word in confidence.
I affirm: This Life is good. This Life is God.
This Life is mine now—and I live it consciously, joyously,
awake.

The Alchemist's Word

"We are chemists in the laboratory of the infinite.
What, then, shall we create?"
E. Holmes

I speak, and something unseen moves.

Not because I command, but because I align.
The Word is not mine—it flows through me, pure and gold,
when my heart is clear.

This is the alchemy: thought forged in fire, emotion stirred
in the crucible, intention folded like light into the living
fabric of form.

Above, the Law—precise, unwavering.
Below, the Love—infinite, undivided.

Together, they answer not what I want, but what I am.

My thoughts are seeds, carried by breath, rooting in the silence
where the invisible becomes real.

The lead of fear transforms when met with the heat of vision,
the solvent of compassion, the tincture of belief.

There is power in me not because I force—but because I *know*.
And what I know shapes what is.

I no longer chase light. I become it.
I no longer beg for peace.
I speak it into the marrow of the moment.

I live in the Goodness now—not as a shield, but as a seeing.
Not to escape the world, but to unveil it in its truest form.

Every element obeys the alchemist who knows the formula:
Love as the fire, Law as the frame, and
the Word as the sacred flame that turns thought into world.

And so I shape, not with struggle, but with stillness—
and the holy gold of knowing that I Am.

The Self-Evidence of Truth

In *The Science of Mind*, Holmes reminds us—drawing from Plotinus—that **Truth does not argue**. Nature does not explain herself; she reveals herself. The stars don't justify their placement. The tree doesn't apologize for its roots. It is **only the human mind**, in its uncertainty, that attempts to debate or prove what already *is*.

Holmes writes of a spiritual realization where we no longer live by effortful argument or proof, but by inner alignment. In this place, **spiritual truth becomes self-evident**, like light entering a darkened room—it doesn't need explanation. It simply transforms.

This is the consciousness we are called to cultivate: not one of strain or convincing, but of **clarity and embodiment**. When we live from the deep truth of who we are—perfect expressions of the One Life—we, like nature, begin to **move with silent authority**.

Let us be like nature: still, radiant, precise. Let us live the truth so clearly that it becomes a demonstration, not a debate.

The Greatest Good

The greatest good is not given—it awakens.
Not in thunder, but in the quiet surge when the soul
remembers its name was never separate from the stars.

The moment comes and the veil lifts—not out there, but in here.
And you see it: Heaven is not a distant realm,
not a reward for suffering quietly.
It is a state of knowing, a flame within
that never needed permission to burn.

To be certain of yourself—not in arrogance, but in *Truth*—
is to walk knowing you are not a fragment but the field itself.
Not a fleeting breath, but breath born of infinity.

You are not aging. You are *unfolding*.
Not falling behind—but becoming exactly what the universe
dreams of when it says yes to life again.

Limitation is a language you no longer speak.
You speak light now. You speak wholeness.
You speak the yes that the cosmos
has always been waiting to echo.

There is no end to your rising. There is no ceiling to
your growth.
You are eternal motion in sacred rhythm—
joy unchained from circumstance.

And what is unhappiness but forgetting?
What is fear but a shadow?
A shadow cast by your own light when you turn away?
Turn back. Face it. Be still.

The universe lives in you as you.
And once you know that, truly, you will never be lost again.

Abundance & Prosperity Reimagined

I used to hold abundance tight,
Measured it in coins, counted each night,
The stacks too small, the needs too tall,
Bound by fear of a future fall.

Anger lingered, like an unpaid debt,
A forgiveness spoken but never fully met—
For scars of loss and trust denied,
Left shadows where my hope would hide.

But then came the shift, a soft, new voice,
Whispering of realms beyond mere choice,
That wealth could stretch past silver's gleam,
Into the boundless, a living dream.

Prosperity, I learned, wore many names,
A dance of love, of peace, unchained,
Health in the body, joy in the soul,
The wealth of knowing that I am whole.

No longer gripped by lack or blame,
The ties that bound, released their claim—
Forgiveness now flowed, true and deep,
A letting go, a soul's leap.

For abundance lives where spirit grows,
In giving freely, where kindness flows.
Now I walk with a fuller view,
Prosperity's face, refreshed, renewed.

No longer tethered to fear's demand,
I feel the wealth within my hand,
In love, in peace, in every breath,
Prosperity redefined, unbound by death.

64

The Spiral of Life

There is no straight line in Spirit—
only the ever-unfolding spiral of becoming.
Like the nautilus shell, we grow from within,
layer upon radiant layer, never abandoning what was,
 but expanding on the Infinite pattern
etched by Divine Intelligence.

Awareness begins at the center—
the still point, where God knows itself as us.
From there, Life whispers outward,
a golden ratio of realization: each turn, each breath,
each "I am" wider, wiser, more whole.

We do not *progress* as mortals do.
We *unfold* like galaxies birthed from light.
The Law receives every thought cast like a seed—
and Love shapes it, softly, surely, into form.

No experience is wasted.
The pain, the peace, the silence between knowing—
all of it spins the arc of our divine architecture.

Holmes wrote: *"We are not bound by precedent,"*
and the spiral agrees.
There is no going back.
Only onward, upward, inward, always Home.

So I walk this spiral path not in haste, but in reverence—
trusting the arc, blessing the curve,
saying yes to the next luminous ring of becoming.

I Move as Truth Moves

I move as Truth moves—
without effort, without argument,
in perfect peace and purpose.

I rest in the stillness where wisdom flows,
needing no defense,
for Light alone discloses.

I live by the Law that governs the stars—
silent, sure, unfolding what already *is*.

The Quiet Knower Within

There is a place beneath the noise
where truth arrives without a word.
Not summoned, not reasoned—
only remembered.

A soft illumination rising from the deep.
Intuition is the whisper of the Infinite
speaking in our own voice—
a knowing older than thought,
carried by the Law that responds
before we speak its name.

It guides without pushing,
reveals without proving.
It is the nudge toward wholeness,
the shimmer of right action
before the mind can question why.

For Spirit does not argue—It unfolds.
It does not compel—It clarifies.
In the quiet, Principle becomes personal,
a compass aligned to the One Life
flowing through all.

When I listen, I hear the echo
of First Cause
stirring possibility in the invisible.

I feel Love shaping my path with intelligence
too vast for logic, yet intimate as breath.

Intuition is the bridge
where heaven meets choice,
where consciousness becomes creation,
where thought becomes form.
The universe leans toward me
as I lean toward it—
two sides of the same awakening.

And in that still communion, I remember
I am not seeking guidance from beyond—
I am uncovering the guidance
that has always moved within.

The Light knows the way. The Law makes it so.
And I, aligned with both, walk the path of Truth revealed—
certain, surrendered, awake to the quiet knower
that never leads me astray.

Moving With What Is

I do not stand apart from life trying to shape it.
I feel it moving through me —
breath finding breath, step meeting ground.

When I am quiet enough, I sense where to lean,
where to soften, where to say yes without effort.
What unfolds does so as I am willing —
present, aligned, awake.

My word does not push forward.
It settles in, like warmth into the hands,
like light into an open room.

I move as life moves — not ahead of it,
not behind it, but within its rhythm.

And here, I rest —
giving myself
to this shared creation,
and it is so.

The Heart of Being

In sacred stillness, all is One,
A golden thread through moon and sun.
No place where Spirit does not live,
No limit to the Love it gives.

It whispers deep within our chest,
A pulse of Peace, a place of rest.
More near than breath, brighter than flame,
The Presence speaks our secret name.

Though clothed in flesh, we shine, we glow —
A truth the wise and mystics know.
These forms, but veils we wear with grace,
Eternal light behind each face.

This cosmos flows with wise design,
A rhythmic dance, a pulse divine.
Its patterns speak in star and seed,
A sacred law to meet each need.

No distant heaven must we find —
The Kingdom lives within the mind.
Through every loving thought we cast,
We shape the future, free the past.

Our words are keys, our thoughts the fire,
They stir the depths, they rise, inspire.
Each silent prayer, each spoken tone
Becomes the life we call our own.

Free agents of the Infinite,
We choose our path, our truth, our light.
And every choice becomes the clay
To shape the soul in conscious play.

We are not bound by time or end,
In death we shift, transform, transcend.
From Life to Life, from dream to star,
The soul remembers who we are.

And so we walk the path of flame,
Awakening to Love's true name.
For freedom calls, and joy reveals
The God within that always heals.

Consent to Co-Creation

I do not command creation.
I consent to it.

Through the words I choose
and the feelings I give them.
Through the knowing
that what I hold as my truth
meets me in form.

I speak carefully—not to persuade Spirit,
but to agree with it.
I let my words, emotions and thoughts
carry the tone of what I am willing to receive.

What moves through me
does not ask to be controlled.
It responds to belief made tender,
to intention softened into trust.

I offer my attention as agreement.
My presence as permission.
And having given my yes in word
and in heart,
I become still—trusting what I have joined
to know its way.

Closing — Becoming & Creative Law

What has been spoken here
was not meant to instruct, but to align.

I have not learned how to shape life.
I have remembered how to agree with it—
in word, in feeling, in belief held gently enough
to receive.

May what I speak arise from listening,
and what I believe be rooted
in the good I am willing to embody.

Let my words be clear without force,
my intentions steady without strain,
and my knowing free
from the need to prove itself.

What is set in motion
does not require my vigilance.
It asks only my integrity.

And so I release the doing
and rest in the allowing—
trusting that what I have joined
will unfold in its own wise time.

Section V — Oneness Embodied

*"Love points the way,
and Law clears the path."*
—Ernest Holmes

Where Spirit Touches Earth

The oak tree is a sermon, the river a prayer—
both born from a silence deeper than sound.

Spirit does not stand apart from nature—
It is the pulse within it.
The whisper in wind, the geometry of snow.

We speak of God, but creation speaks as God—
Each petal, a syllable of the Infinite's voice.

When I awaken, it is not *above* nature I rise, but *into* it—
finally hearing what has always been said.

The Sacred in the Ordinary

I do not have to look
beyond this moment
to find what is holy.

It meets me in the weight of my body—
in breath moving without asking,
in the quiet intelligence of my hands
opening and closing without thought.

Nothing here is waiting
to become sacred.
The ordinary **IS** sacred.

The cup warms my palms.
The floor holds my feet.
The chair receives my weight.
My spine rises and settles.
My pulse keeps time without instruction.

Skin meets air. Sound enters and leaves.
Light rests on surfaces and moves on.

The day offers itself without explanation,
and my body knows how to belong to it.
I am not separate from this simplicity.

I am included in every movement—
every contact, every breath taken and released.

Here, in what I almost overlooked,
Spirit remembers itself not as idea, not as visitor,
but as this living moment
wearing my name.

The Body Is Not Separate

This body is not solid.
It is listening.

Energy moving close enough to touch—
warmth passing between us,
presence meeting presence
without needing words.

I feel you before I name you.
A shift in the room. A softening.
A quiet recognition that something alive
has entered my field.

Nothing stops at the skin.
What I feel travels—through breath shared,
through a glance held a moment longer,
through the subtle exchange of being seen.

My body knows how to receive and how to offer.
It responds with gentleness, with openness,
with the simple courage of connection.

In every meeting, energy speaks—
attention flowing, care awakening,
belonging remembering itself.

I am not contained here.
I am participating in a living exchange
where Spirit recognizes Spirit as us.

The World Is Listening

I no longer feel alone inside the day.
Something meets me before I speak—
a soft attention, a readiness already awake.

When I enter a room gently, the air seems to notice.
When I slow, the world slows with me.
What moves through me moves outward—
not as effort, but as tone, as presence
felt more than seen.

A glance carries warmth. Stillness carries meaning.
Even silence has a texture that touches what surrounds it.
There is an intimacy here beyond words—
a quiet communion where life recognizes itself
through us.

I am not sending anything out.
I am participating in a shared awareness
already listening, already responding.

In this tender exchange, nothing is separate.
Everything belongs to the same listening heart.

Seeing Through the Eyes of Love

When I look with love, nothing is distant.
Edges soften. The sharpness of judgment
loosens its hold.

I see more than form —
I sense the life moving beneath appearances,
asking only to be met.

Love does not fix what it sees. It recognizes.
In its gaze, even what is wounded
remembers its belonging.

Even what is hidden feels safe enough
to emerge.
Through love, I do not stand apart.
I stand within — inside the same pulse,
the same breath, looking back at itself.

What I see changes
because *how* I see has changed.
And in this seeing,
the world becomes familiar again —
not as something to manage,
but as something already held.

The Earth Knows My Name

I am a visitor here,
Spirit moving in physical form—
a sacred guest learning how to touch the world.

The earth receives me not because I remain,
but because I am one with All.

My breath meets the air as kin recognizing kin.
My feet greet the ground as memory answering memory.
The earth knows my name because it was spoken
from Source.

God lives within me—not separate, not diminished.
I have awakened to my Oneness with all.

Trees do not ask how long I will stay.
Stones do not question my purpose.
They recognize that I will always be—
just not in physical form.

And I remember, standing here for a moment,
that I am not foreign to what I pass through.

I walk gently, knowing I will leave—
and knowing I am known all the same.

The Holy Appears as This

I no longer search for what is sacred.
Everything around me is sacred.

In the face before me.
In the sound that interrupts.
In the moment that embodies
and blooms.

Nothing arrives outside the Holy.
Nothing waits to be blessed.
The ache, the laughter,
the unfinished thought—
all carry the same belonging.

Spirit does not visit this world.
It inhabits it—fully, without exception.

I do not divide my days
into worthy and unworthy.
No matter the situation, I am worthy.

Here, nothing is excluded.
Nothing is elsewhere.
The Holy appears as this.

Love Moves Through Me

Love does not arise as feeling.
It is not moved by preference
or pulled by need.

It is the steadiness that remains
when emotion passes.
I recognize it as openness without demand—
as presence that does not choose sides,
as regard that does not withdraw.

Love does not react. It allows.
It meets what is without resistance,
without requirement to be different.

When I embody my Oneness,
love moves as clarity—
as the simple refusal to divide.

Nothing is excluded.
Nothing is negotiated.
This is not human affection.

It is divine inclusion.
And when it moves through me,
the world is met as it is—
already whole.

No One Is Outside This

I experience life from where I stand—
through this breath, this body,
this unfolding moment.

Others move through their own becoming,
guided by choices I do not make for them
and truths I do not need to hold.
And still, nothing is separate.

What I feel touches the whole
without erasing anyone else's path.
I honor the way each life meets itself—
in joy or struggle, in certainty or doubt—
without needing it to look like mine.

I am responsible not for another's journey,
but for how I arrive in my own.
How I listen. How I allow.
How gently I move through what is shared.

No one is outside of belonging.
No one is excluded from the field of life.
We do not live the same story.
We live the same presence—
each of us meeting it in our own way.

I Am One With the Living Spirit of All Creation

I am one with the living Spirit
that breathes in all things—
in roots, in stars,
in stillness.

I move as nature moves,
in sacred rhythm, effortless and aligned.

My thoughts shape beauty
as Spirit shapes form—
unseen and visible as One.

Closing — Oneness Embodied

What has been revealed here
was never meant to lift me out of the world,
but to return me to it awake.

I do not leave this knowing to be remembered later.
I carry it as presence—into movement, into encounter,
into the ordinary holiness of living.

May I honor my own experience
without diminishing another's.
May I walk gently, knowing that Oneness
does not erase difference, but holds it.

Infinite Love, not as feeling, but as order,
teach me to trust Your way.
Where I resist, soften me.
Where I doubt, steady me.

May I align my life with what already knows
how to hold all things together.
Nothing needs to be added to make this true.
Nothing needs to be removed to make it whole.

Spirit has not been found—
it has been recognized as what has always been here,
appearing as all things, including me.

And so I rest in what is embodied,
trusting that what has been known will continue
to live itself through me.

Section VI — Spirit Made Visible

*"Spirit becomes visible
where it touches the human heart."*
—Joel Goldsmith

The Unity of Spirit and Nature

The relationship between spiritual consciousness and nature is not one of separation but of **intimacy and identity**. In *The Science of Mind*, Holmes teaches that Spirit and Its creation are one—**form is the result of thought**, and nature is Spirit clothed in time and space.

When we walk in a forest, we do not leave spirituality behind. Instead, we walk through the **embodied presence of God**. The rustling leaves, the changing light, the precision of a bee's flight—all are expressions of **divine intention** manifest.

Spiritual consciousness awakens us not to "something else," but to a deeper **recognition** of what already is. To see nature rightly is to see God's mind in motion. And to live in spiritual alignment is to know that our thoughts, like seeds, can shape the world—just as surely as rain shapes stone.

We are not apart from creation. We are the voice, the hand, and the heart of it.

To honor nature is to honor ourselves, and to awaken is to remember: **we are creation remembering its Source**.

Compassion as Our Moral Foundation

"Compassion is the basis of morality."
A. Schopenhauer

I feel the pain of others as my own.
In empathy, I discover morality.
Compassion guides the awakened mind.

Where pity begins, cruelty ends.
The heart that softens holds the world together.

Let me not ask what one deserves—
only what they need.
Let me be the shelter I seek.

Identity of Love

Love is not something I give away,
but the truth of what I am —
a pulse within the Infinite Heart.

No place is untouched. No soul is lost.
Love knows the way where no path is marked.

My life is one with God — not someday, not after —
but now, as breath, as light, as every sacred matter.
In this Unity, I rest. In this Peace, I stand.

The world is met by the Love I embody.
The trees receive it without question.
The sky reflects it without end.
The song of the earth moves through me
as its own expression.

What I am circulates as Grace —
**one expression of life and love
made conscious**.

Love Does Not Harm

Love does not wound to prove a point.
It does not use power to quiet another voice,
nor truth to diminish.

Love does not take what cannot be freely given,
but gives freely in the aid of another.

It moves with discernment that does not need
to oppose.
It carries a knowing that settles
rather than confronts.

When love is present,
positive possibilities abound.
Choice is available and allowed.
Time is not an issue.

Love chooses care as its natural expression—
for life, for dignity, for what cannot be restored
once broken.

This is not restraint imposed.
It is understanding.
And where love is allowed to guide the way,
no one is required to be diminished
for another to stand.

Hold Love in Reverence with Life

Love does not move without honoring listening.
It notices what rests in its care—
a word, a moment, a shared silence,
the weight of being trusted.

What is spoken is shaped by awareness.
What is offered is given with attention.
What is received is met gently,
as something living.

Reverence is not caution. It is affection awake.
I feel it in how I pause, in how I choose, in how I sense
the unseen threads my actions touch.

Love does not crowd.
It leaves space. It honors enough.
It moves without taking more than is needed.

This is how love tends to the world—
not through rule or force,
but through presence
that knows what it is holding.

Love Is Without Judgment

Love does not judge.
It allows choice to remain possible.
It sees clearly without condemning,
and holds space without collapse.

Boundaries arise not as punishment,
but as care—a way of saying
this matters.

Love does not force alignment.
It creates conditions where alignment
can be chosen.
Here, possibility stays open.
Movement remains available.

Life is not cornered into defense.
I can say no without closing my heart.
I can hold a boundary without withdrawing love.
This is not leniency.
It is respect for the dignity of choice.

Love keeps the field intact—
wide enough for growth,
clear enough to protect what is precious.

What Love Makes Possible

Love does not promise ease.
It opens space.
It makes room for listening
where reaction once lived,
for understanding without fear
or doubt.

Because love is present, something softens.
Because love remains, something new
can begin.

Possibility does not rush in.
It waits for willingness.
Here, choice widens. Time relaxes.
There is only this moment.

Love does not decide for me.
It makes it possible for me to decide what may yet emerge.
This is what love offers—not outcomes, but openings.

The Weight Love Carries

Love does not carry weight.
It carries presence.
It does not measure, or assign, or require.

Love remains—unchanged
by what is chosen or refused.

When I become aware,
it is not because love has asked more of me,
but because I have noticed
what was already here.

Love does not hold consequence.
It holds space.
It allows every movement,
every learning, every return.

If something steadies me,
it is not obligation, but recognition—
a quiet sensing of what aligns
and what does not.

Love does not ask me to be better.
It does not demand repair.
It simply stays.

And in that staying,
I find myself willing—
not from pressure, but from belonging.

To Live What I Know

I do not need more understanding.
What I know is already sufficient
to live from.

The invitation is simple:
to let my life reflect my awareness.
Not perfectly. Not loudly.
But faithfully.

It shows itself in kindness—
in how I speak, how I choose,
how I remain when leaving
would be easier.

I practice alignment in ordinary ways,
letting care move through me
without needing to be noticed.

This is not a vow.
It is a direction.
To live what I know is to let love
take the lead, and allow it
to be seen.

And in doing so, I find
that knowing has become
a way of being.

Closing — Spirit Made Visible

The world does not need more noise. It needs presence.
It needs those willing to let love take form—
not as emotion, not as ideal, but as lived intelligence.

Love is not something to be admired from a distance
or spoken about endlessly.
It is meant to be inhabited,
not something to worship, but something to be.

To live aligned is not to convince the world,
but to meet it with steadiness,
with clarity, with kindness
that does not announce itself.

My life is one with God.
Not as belief, but as fact.
And love moves through me not as effort,
but as expression—touching what it touches,
shaping what it meets.

This is not metaphor. It is participation.
And when love is lived this way, quietly, faithfully,
the world responds—
not because it was told to,
but because law has been allowed to work.

Section VII — Resting in the Heart of Being

"Words are the most powerful force available to humanity.
Through them, the unseen moves into form."
—Ernest Holmes

The Word That Knows Itself

Before I speak, Spirit is already listening—
not waiting, not deciding, but tenderly responding,
as breath responds to lungs, as echo answers sound.

I do not persuade the Infinite.
I lean into what already is.
My word is not hope flung outward,
nor wish shaped like prayer.

It is recognition, a loving remembering spoken aloud.
What I name, I consent to. What I claim, I inhabit.
What I affirm, the universe gently arranges itself around,
as if it has been waiting for my yes.

There is no delay in Spirit,
only my willingness to agree with love
and let it be enough.

I release effort. I release force.
I release the need to see the bridge
before stepping onto it,
trusting it will rise to meet me
step by step.

The Law does not judge my certainty—
it meets it with patience, with kindness, with grace.
And so I choose my word as one chooses a path at dawn:
quietly, deliberately, with trust deeper than proof
and softer than fear.

I speak from alignment, not desire.
From truth, not fear.
And what is spoken moves into form
without struggle, without resistance,
without apology—as naturally as light
finding the morning and staying.

For the Word was never separate from the world.
It is the world remembering how to appear,
and welcoming itself home through me.

The Surrendering...a soul ready to remember

There comes a moment—not in thunder, but in the hush
between thoughts—
when the self you built begins to dissolve like mist in morning
light.

It is not loss. It is unveiling.
It is not weakness. It is *trust*.
You were never meant to carry the weight of illusion
when your wings were made for sky.

Let it fall—the name that bound you,
the roles you mastered, the ache of not-enough.
There is no shame in shedding.
The seed splits to awaken.
The stars burn to shine.

To become who you are is to *un-become*
what you were never meant to be.
This is the holy undoing. The sacred unravel.
At that moment you stop steering and start *surrendering*.

Faith is not the absence of fear, it is the song you sing
while walking into the unknown,
knowing the ground will rise to meet you because it always has.

You are not lost. You are opening.
And what opens is the heart of God
beating in time with your own.

You are not becoming someone new —
you are becoming someone *true*.
This path is not upward. It is *inward*.

To the flame, to the well, to the Word that spoke you into
being.
And when the world asks, "Who are you now?"
You smile like the moon smiles at tide, and say:
"I am what Love looks like when it lets go."

Nothing Is Required

Nothing is being asked of me now.
No clarity to reach. No lesson to complete.
No threshold to cross.

What has been learned has already returned me
to what I am—not separate, not striving, not alone.
Breath arrives without effort, as Love always does.

The body knows how to belong to this moment.
I feel the quiet agreement between myself
and what unifies all things—a soft alignment
where nothing is opposed and nothing is withheld.

I am in this moment. I do not shape it.
I allow what I know to live as kindness,
as patience, as presence.

Oneness is not an idea. Love is not a task.
They are the ground I stand on
without needing to remember how.

And from this ground,
nothing more is required.

Before Thought

Before the word arrives, there is this—
a quiet knowing that does not need to speak.

Before the name forms,
there is presence meeting itself
without question.

It feels like ease in the chest,
like breath finding its way home,
like being held without asking
by what has always been here.

Nothing is missing. Nothing is out of place.
I do not need to understand this stillness to trust it.
I recognize it as the same presence that has carried me
through every moment—
now revealed without effort, without thought.

In this space, clarity is not an answer.
It is a sense of belonging.
And in that belonging, I rest
before thought needs to begin.

Held

I am not holding myself together.
I am resting in what has always been whole.

God is not outside this moment.
God is within my breath, my body,
the quiet that surrounds me.

I feel it in the way breath returns,
in the way my body knows how to settle,
in the way I am connected to everything
without effort.

Nothing here is separate. Nothing is unsupported.
I do not have to stay alert to remain safe.
I do not have to strive to belong.

What holds me is the same Presence
that holds all things—unchanging, unconditional,
nearer than thought.

I am held because I am part of what holds.
And in this knowing, I rest.

Still Enough

Stillness does not mean nothing is moving.
It means all is possibility.

Breath comes and goes.
The heart keeps its rhythm.
Life continues.

I am still enough to feel
how everything belongs—
the sound in the room,
the light on the wall,
the pulse within my chest.

Nothing needs to be fixed.
Nothing needs to arrive.
In this stillness, I am not waiting.
I am present.

God is not elsewhere when things grow quiet.
God is here—in the ease of this moment,
in the connection that does not break
when I stop reaching.

Still enough to notice. Still enough to trust.
Still enough to let life be itself through me.

No Distance

There is no distance between myself
and what I am seeking.
What I once reached for has been here—
quietly, without demand.

I do not cross a threshold to arrive.
I soften and notice I am already included.
The space I thought existed
was made of attention, not absence.

Nothing stands between me
and the life I am living.
Nothing stands between me
and God.

There is no edge where I end
and something else begins—
only relationship resting in itself.

I am not meeting the Infinite from afar.
I am within it, and it is within me,
without distance, without division,
without effort.

Silence Knows My Name

I do not speak to be known.
Silence already recognizes me—
not as something distant,
but as its own.

Not by history. Not by role.
Not by what I have done.
By presence.

Before I answer, before I choose,
before I remember myself,
I am known.

Silence does not ask
who I am becoming.
It rests with who I am—
with the part of me
that has never needed
to change.

Nothing needs to be said,
and everything is held
as truth.

Closing — Resting in the Heart of Being

Creative Intelligence moves quietly
through thought and word,
without hurry, without strain.

I rest in this knowing—
that responsibility need not carry fear,
and creation need not begin with effort.

May what I speak arise from truth
already present.
May what I imagine be worthy of form
because it is born of love.
May what I create serve more than myself
by remembering we are never separate.

I do not ask to be capable.
I allow what is already so to move through me.
And in this resting,
my words become blessings.

And all of this

was never separate from you.

Section VIII — As the Journey Continues

"Spirit becomes visible
where it touches the human heart."
—Joel Goldsmith

The Way of Love

Love points the way, and Law clears the path,
Through Christ Consciousness, I embrace my task.
A vessel of grace, to all I meet,
I offer kindness, both simple and sweet.

A smile, a word, a moment to share,
To show the world that Love is there.
In shelters of hope or hands that feed,
I serve with compassion; I honor the need.

For Love stands tall as kindness and care,
A mirror of Christ, so pure, so rare.
In humble respect, I listen and hear,
Each voice, each heart, with empathy's ear.

I forgive the past; no resentment I hold,
For Love releases, makes the broken whole.
To love others deeply, I start with me,
Self-care and kindness set my spirit free.

When Love fades, judgment fills the void,
I demand the world conform to my voice.
Self-centered, I stray, blinded by pride,
And compassion retreats where ego resides.

Yet Love redeems, its promise stands true:
"Love is patient, Love is kind, in all you do."
It keeps no record, it holds no score,
It seeks the truth and nothing more.

Love always protects, trusts, and stays,
A light unwavering through all our days.
It hopes, it perseveres, it never departs,
A sacred fire within our hearts.

So, daily I choose to walk in this way,
To be Love in action, come what may.
For in Love's embrace, the world is healed,
Its power revealed, its promise sealed.

One Life, One Love

I send Love to the world—not as a gift apart,
but as the truth of what I am—
a pulse within the Infinite Heart.

No place is untouched. No soul is lost.
Love knows the way where no path is marked.

My life is one with God—not someday, not after—
but now, as breath, as light, as every sacred matter.

In this Unity, I rest. In this Peace, I stand.
The world is healed by the Love in my hands.

The trees receive it without question.
The sky reflects it without end.
The song of the earth is the song I extend.

This Love I send returns to me—
a circle of divine embrace.
For what I give, I am,
I know: one Life, one Love, one Grace.

A Call by the Sea

By the edge of the sea, where the waves touch the soul,
A voice calls forth, whispering: *Be whole.*
For within each heart, a light so divine,
Waits to be nurtured, to flourish, to shine.

No walls of dogma, no limits confine,
The power within us is greater than time.
Infinite spirit, the force of creation,
Moves through us all, with boundless elation.

The world shall awaken, in love and in grace,
We are the vessels, the sacred embrace.
To heal and to serve, to teach and to grow,
This is our mission, the truth we must show.

We are not small, but vast as the sky,
Connected in spirit, we never can die.
Through every hand that reaches to give,
Flows the one life, the power to live.

Let us march forward, as beacons of light,
Turning shadows today, with love as our might.
The kingdom of heaven is not far away—
It lives in our hearts, it blooms in today.

By the sea we are called, to rise and to be
The fullness of God's own eternity.
For in every soul, the divine plan is spun,
We are not separate—*we are all one.*

Inspired by Ernest Holmes's The Sermon by the Sea which tells us that each of us carries within the potential for divine expression and that our purpose is to serve humanity by bringing forth love, healing, and spiritual awareness. I wrote this after contemplating my reading of it and what it said to me.

There Is Wisdom in Restraint

*"To desire immortality is to desire the perpetuation
of a great mistake."*
A. Schopenhauer

Let me not beg for forever.
Eternity is not the answer if I do not love the moment.

I do not wish to repeat blindly what I have not yet understood.
Wisdom chooses enough.

Life is not about endlessness, but about depth.
I want truth, not time.

The World We Heal by Loving

In an era where fear travels faster than truth, where division seems louder than unity, the words of Ernest Holmes ring like a bell through the noise: *"My life is one with God."* And from that truth flows another: *"I send Love to the world."*

These two declarations—simple yet vast—form the spiritual axis upon which a new world might turn. As mystics and metaphysicians, we are not passive spectators of reality. We are co-creators, consciousness in motion. And every thought, every choice, every radiant act of love is a vibration that joins the great field of becoming.

Love as the Only Real Power
Holmes does not speak of love sentimentally. His is not the love of fleeting emotion, but of **principle**—Love as **Law**, Love as **Cause**, Love as the **nature of Reality** itself. When we affirm that we send Love to the world, we are not merely offering goodwill—we are aligning with **the most creative force in the cosmos**.

To love the world, in Holmes's vision, is to heal it—not by fixing, but by **recognizing**. Recognizing the God-nature in all things. Recognizing the perfect pattern behind appearances. And by doing so, we become **living instruments** of peace, clarity, and grace.

The Practice of Oneness

When we say, "My life is one with God," we are not making a wish. We are making a **claim**. A remembrance. We are speaking from the eternal place within us where duality has never existed.

This Oneness is not earned. It is not bestowed. It simply is. Our spiritual practice, then, is not to *achieve* connection—it is to *awaken to it*. Meditation, affirmative prayer, silence, and conscious living become tools not to reach God, but to release everything that obscures the **truth that we are already one**. From that awareness, Love flows effortlessly—not from effort, but from identity.

Becoming a Healing Presence
To love the world is to look upon it with unwavering **spiritual vision**. To see beyond war, scarcity, or sorrow—and to hold, *"a silent expectancy of good."* Not as denial, but as dominion.

When we embody Oneness and radiate Love, we become a **vortex of healing**. We enter a room and peace expands. We speak, and calm arises. Not because of our personality, but because of our alignment.

This is the mystical call of our time: to love not just personally, but cosmically. To affirm that every life is part of our own, and every moment an opportunity to bless.

Final Thoughts

You have not arrived somewhere new.
You have returned
to what has always been
moving through you.

Let what you have remembered find its way
into how you listen, how you choose,
how you stand within the world.

Carry nothing special. Prove nothing.
Walk gently. Speak truly.

Trust the quiet law that knows how to become
without your effort.
What you are has never been separate
from what is.

Go now—not as one who knows,
but as one who belongs.

About the Author

Dr. Linda Hildebrant is a spiritual writer and contemplative poet whose work explores silence, presence, oneness, and the lived experience of the sacred. Walking a conscious spiritual path since the mid-1980s, her writing is shaped by mysticism, metaphysical philosophy, psychology, and a deep trust in Divine Intelligence revealed through lived experience rather than doctrine.

Raised Southern Baptist, Linda began an expansive spiritual inquiry in 1985 that led her beyond inherited belief into direct exploration. Over the years, she has studied and engaged with a wide range of spiritual and philosophical traditions, including metaphysics, New Thought, Religious Science, Zen Buddhism, Theosophy, and contemporary integral and mystical teachings. These influences inform her work not as systems to follow, but as lenses through which truth may be encountered and embodied.

Linda's writing is not offered as instruction, nor as a path to master. It is an invitation—to pause, to listen, and to remember what has always been present beneath the surface of daily life. Her words create space rather than answers, trusting that insight arises naturally when the mind quiets and the heart opens. She writes for seekers drawn to spirituality that is experiential, embodied, and quietly transformative.

In parallel with her spiritual work, Linda earned a Ph.D. in Organization and Management with an emphasis in

Leadership. Her doctoral research explored the intersection of spirituality, psychology, and ethics, culminating in a dissertation titled *Spiritual Intelligence: Is It Related to a Leader's Level of Ethical Development?* This work reflects her long-standing interest in how inner awareness shapes outer expression—how consciousness, values, and lived integrity inform the way we lead, create, and relate.

Linda is the creator of **SacredBeyondWords.com**, a contemplative space devoted to poetry, meditations, devotional readings, and reflections inspired by the Universal Presence that lives in us, through us, and as us. The site serves as a sanctuary for spiritual seekers, mystics, creatives, and all who sense that awakening is less about becoming something new and more about remembering what is already true.

The Sacred Return When Life Remembers Itself is her first published poetry collection, offering a contemplative journey told through poetry, silence, and sacred reflection. Like all of her work, it is not meant to be completed, but returned to— allowing what is remembered to find its way gently into how one lives.

When Life Remembers Itself is
a contemplative journey told through
poetry, silence, and sacred reflection.

This collection is not meant to instruct or persuade.
It is an invitation—to pause, to listen, and to remember
what has always been present beneath the noise of becoming.

Moving through themes of stillness, awakening, oneness,
love, creative law, and embodied presence,
these poems trace a path that is not linear, but inward.
They speak to the quiet moments where insight arises
without effort, where truth does not announce itself, and
where the soul recognizes what it has never truly forgotten.

Written for those
who sense that life is more
appearances—and gentler than striving—
this book offers space rathen answers,
presence rathan conclusions.

Read slowly.
Leave room between the words.
Let what is remembered find its way into how you live.

This is not a book to finish.
It is a place to return to—
for what you are seeking
has been listening all along.